A Pitara of Love

About the Author

Ameya Aneja is currently a Grade 12 student at Delhi Public School, R.K. Puram. She lives in New Delhi with her family. She is a strong advocate for women in STEM especially in the field of aerospace and engineering, where she has won several prestigious national and international competitions. She is an avid reader and is also the author of 'Twice the Twist', a bestselling and award winning mystery fiction novella that she authored and published when she was 11 years old. When Ameya is not writing, she is leading innovative research projects in astrophysics and engineering, while mentoring young girls to hone their passion for aerospace. Through this book, she combines her love for cultural traditions, the culinary arts and her deep connection with her grandmother, a truly heartfelt tribute. Inspired by her grandmother's journey, she is committed to promoting women's health and empowering women suffering from breast cancer. She also loves playing the piano and mastering complex compositions. She continues to maintain a strong academic record and has been one of the top students of her class.

A Pitara of Love

Ameya Aneja

ZORBA BOOKS

ZORBA BOOKS

Published by Zorba Books, August 2024
Website: www.zorbabooks.com
Email: info@zorbabooks.com
Author Name: Ameya Aneja
Copyright ©: Ameya Aneja

Title: A Pitara of Love

Printbook ISBN: 978-93-5896-966-5
Ebook ISBN: 978-93-5896-015-0

Zorba Books Pvt. Ltd. (opc)
Sushant Arcade,
Next to Courtyard Marriot,
Sushant Lok 1, Gurgaon – 122009, India

Printed by Manipal Technologies Limited
A1 & A2 Shivalli Industrial Area Manipal Udupi, Karnataka – 57610

*Dedicated to my nani, whose love flavors
every moment of my life.*

Contents

Acknowledgements

First and foremost, my heartfelt thanks to my grandmother, who inspires me everyday and whose kitchen is a place of learning, laughter and love. Your wisdom and culinary expertise have been the foundation of this book. I am greatly indebted to my parents, especially my mother, for her unwavering support and great ideas.

Special thanks to Vandana Aunty for sharing her delectable Kashmiri recipes and to Kalpana didi, for being a constant help in the kitchen. I would also like to thank my Nanu, who shares my love for reading, for his invaluable suggestions that have been instrumental in shaping this book. I am blessed to receive love and affection from my Dadu and Dadi. To my friends, thank you for your encouragement and feedback that kept me motivated. I am also grateful to my publisher, Zorba Books Pvt. Ltd and my editors. I also thank my Principal and English teachers at D.P.S R.K.Puram for their guidance and encouragement throughout this journey.

Finally, to all the readers, thank you for opening this book and sharing the love and memories that have been poured in every page. I hope this collection brings joy to your kitchen, just as they have to mine.

Ameya Aneja
July 2024

Prologue

A Journey through Taste and Time

April, 2023. What I thought would be a mundane day at my grandma's house turned out to be the most unforgettable day, leading to the creation of this book. The relentless downpour set the scene as my grandmother and I sat in her cozy verandah, sipping steaming cups of tea and savoring our crisp samosas dipped in tangy chutney. The fresh, earthy smell of the rain accompanied with the lush green leaves thriving in her garden marked a good beginning to the evening.

Just then, this tranquil moment was interrupted by my grandfather's voice, "The phone has been ringing for so long, why aren't you answering?" My grandmother hastily put down her cup and rushed to pick up the phone, leaving me to ponder whose call it was that disrupted our enchanting tea party. When she returned, I could see her eyes twinkling with delight and excitement. I couldn't help but ask, 'What is it?'

She exclaimed, 'Guess what? It's Pimmi masi's 75th birthday next month and we are planning a grand celebration!' It took me a minute to remember which masi she was referring to - such nicknames are all too common in Punjabi households. My grandmother was born into a large, loving and close knit family with seven siblings including herself, who shared a strong bond with an exceptional understanding of each other.

The next few days, my grandmother's house buzzed with excitement as the party preparations began in full swing. There were frantic calls to her sisters to decide the theme, venue, guest list and numerous visits to the local market to stock up on groceries, party decorations and most important of all, order her sister's favourite chocolate birthday cake. After much deliberation, it was decided to organise a potluck for Pimmi Masi's birthday at my grandmother's house. Each sister was to bring one dish to the celebration. 'Good for me and my cousins, they are all exceptional chefs', I said to myself. Planning the menu for this potluck was a task they took very seriously. Each morning, as the landline rang, my nani would gather her notebook and pencil, sitting diligently at the table to discuss the menu with her sisters. For me, this phone call was an unwelcome alarm waking me from my deep slumber, but for my nani, it meant an hour of thorough planning and nostalgia. I often overheard these conversations as they reminisced about masi's favorite childhood snacks and desserts. The stories they shared transported me back in time, to a simpler era where the kitchen was the heart of the home.

One afternoon, after her second menu planning call of the day, she turned to me and said, 'I need you to find my recipe book, Ameya. It has a very special recipe of Sindhi Kadhi that your masi used to love.'

That afternoon, I rummaged through all her drawers and cupboards, but to no avail. Just when I was about to give up, I spotted a tin cookie box buried under a huge pile of her history textbooks. Thinking I was about to taste some delicious cookies, I tugged at it with all my might and pulled it out from the rubble of books. On opening it, I was overcome with mixed feelings. On one hand, I was disappointed for not having found any cookies in the box, while on the other, I was overjoyed to find what seemed like my grandmother's recipe book. A blue, leather bound diary with yellow worn out pages, filled with handwritten recipes, notes and recipe cuttings from various magazines and newspapers which she had meticulously collected over the years. As I proudly handed it to nani, she smiled and said, 'Ah, this book is like a treasure trove of memories for me. Today, we're going to add a new memory.'

The house was filled with the tantalizing aromas of spices and simmering pots as me and nani set to work on the Sindhi Kadhi. Those two hours cooking with her were an absolute adventure: She was like Santa and I was her little helper, handing her ingredients and utensils, as and when she demanded while she taught me the delicate balance of flavors and the importance of patience. As we prepared the dish, she shared stories of her childhood - how she and her sisters would sneak into the kitchen to taste the dishes while they were being prepared, pilfering their favorite snacks, the mischievous pranks they played on each other and their mother, and the simple joys of growing up together.

The day of the party arrived, and my nani's home was a hive of activity as we hurriedly rushed to decorate the precious dish in a beautiful china bowl. As everyone arrived, I could see the sisters gathering, each carrying a dish, their faces glowing with excitement and love. One brought Jalebis, another got Pani Puri, and soon the table was filled with a spread of dishes that spoke volumes about their past.

When masi saw the Sindhi Kadhi, her excitement knew no bounds. She hugged nani tightly and said, 'This is the taste of our childhood'. The room filled with laughter, lively banter and fun stories as the sisters recounted fond memories of time spent together, their joy immeasurable as they tasted each dish.

That evening, surrounded by family and the comforting aroma of home-cooked food, I realized the essence of our culinary heritage. It wasn't about the recipes- it was about the love and thought that was poured into perfecting each dish. Cooking the Sindhi Kadhi with nani, hearing her stories and seeing the big smile on her face is one of my most treasured memories to this day.

It was this experience that inspired me to pen down our culinary secrets and the stories behind each dish, to preserve and celebrate them for future generations. And so, with a heart full of love and a treasure trove of recipes, 'A Pitara of Love' was born. A tribute to the woman who taught me the secret ingredient to any dish is the love that goes into making it.

'Doli Ki Roti'

Cultural Significance

Doli ceremony is one of the most sentimental wedding rituals in India, which represents the bride's departure from her paternal home to her husband's home. In ancient times, the bride would be carried in a 'doli' or a wooden palanquin from her paternal home to her new abode. Doli ki Roti or a 'Bride's gift from Multan', is a delicacy originating from the Multan region in Pakistan. According to many folktales, once the girl of the house got married in a typical Indian marriage setting, as part of her farewell, the girl's family prepared 'Doli ki Roti' for her long journey to her in laws house, as the dish was believed to remain fresh for days due to a special fermentation process. It is usually served with dry lentil stuffing.

Background

When I first asked my fragile grandmother about her infamous Doli ki Roti recipe, the sparkle in her eyes and sudden leap of excitement made me realise the significance of this dish, entrenched in her core memory. The typical hot, humid Delhi summers in the 1960s in my grandmother's childhood home, a traditional Indian courtyard house, would be incomplete without the wafting earthy scent of the traditional 'Doli ki Roti', which children and adults alike would impatiently wait for. One of the superstitions associated with this dish, however, was the fact that women were barred from entering the kitchen if they had their periods during the making of this dish, something my grandmother found very confusing and irrational. She would often argue with her mother trying to reason about such unfounded beliefs and how it was time to not get blinded by such superstitions.

Despite the fervour surrounding its preparation, the name of the dish being cooked was guarded with utmost secrecy like confidential information eagerly waiting to be discovered. It was believed that revealing the name prematurely would inhibit the fermentation of the dough. Regardless of the secrecy, the atmosphere was always filled with a sense of anticipation which could only mean one thing: a grand 'Doli ki Roti' feast!

The dough was always prepared meticulously at night as a sanctified ritual and kept covered, like treasure, as an effort to protect it from eager eyes that could impede its fermentation process. Early in the morning, my maternal great grandmother would ensure the dough had risen and that would mark a flurry of activity as each telephone in the local neighbourhood started ringing, with an invitation to the splendid 'Doli ki Roti' feast. Once the roti was ready, people from far and wide thronged to my grandmother's house with their little steel tiffins, like toddlers wistfully staring at the sweets in a canteen, waiting to devour the scrumptious dish.

'Doli ki Roti' was more than just a culinary delight; it was a celebration with loved ones and the community, creating memories that my grandmother treasures to this day.

🕑 **Preparation time: 1 day**
🍲 **Cooking time: 4 hours**
🛎 **Serves: 25 rotis**

Ingredients

3 tbsp Khaskhas (poppyseed)
2 pieces Dalchini (cinnamon)
10 Cloves
½ Jaifal (nutmeg)
3 Big black elaichi (cardamom)
500 gms Chana dal (split chickpeas)
1 litre Water
2 kg Wheat flour
1 tsp Jeera (cumin seeds)
¼ tsp hing (asafoetida)
1 tsp red chilli powder
1 tsp dhania powder (coriander seed powder)
1 tsp amchoor powder (dry mango powder)
½ tsp Sugar
2 tsp Salt

Procedure

1. Take a heavy bottomed utensil with a small mouth. Boil 750 ml of water on low flame for 7-10 minutes.
2. Wrap Khaskhas, Dalchini, Clove, Jaifal, Big black elaichi and 3 tbsp of chana dal in a muslin cloth and tie it and add it to the boiling water.
3. Let it boil at least 4-5 times.
4. Switch off gas. Cover the mouth with a lid so that no air escapes.
5. Wrap in a blanket and keep it untouched for 24 hours.
6. Next day, at the same time, see if bubbles are there, then strain the water and heat lightly.
7. Add ½ kg atta (flour), mix to get a thin batter.
8. Again cover with a blanket and leave for 2 hours.
9. After 2 hours, the flour will ferment and rise to become fluffy.
10. Add rest of the flour with warm water, add ½ tsp salt, sugar, mix well and cover.
11. After 2 hours, it will ferment and rise.
12. Prepare the filling, by first boiling the chana dal.
13. Heat some oil in a pan, once hot add the hing, jeera, rest of spices, salt and the boiled chana dal. Mix nicely and coarsely mash the dal for the filling. Cool the mixture.
14. Make small balls of the dough and create a hollow depression to stuff the filling. Roll rotis with your hand and put on a sheet and cover.
15. Continue this process till the entire flour is rolled and covered.
16. Deep fry in oil, cool and store.
17. Can be eaten hot or at room temperature.
18. Enjoy!

'Phirni'

Cultural Significance

Having originated in Ancient Persia or the Middle east, Phirni or 'the Food of Angels' is a simple yet exquisite dessert popular in North Indian and Pakistani cuisines. Believed to have been introduced to India by the Mughals, it is also known as Fereni in Iran. Primarily made of milk and rice, it is garnished with an array of dry fruits like raisins, cashews and almonds to give it an exquisite 'shahi' touch. Phirni is a royal dessert that is widely enjoyed during Ramadan and other Eid festivities.

Background

The other day while I was visiting my grandmother's house, I was chided for glancing over my phone all the time. 'Be more participative,' said my grandparents as I scrolled absentmindedly, detached from the ongoing discussion about the menu of a party they were hosting. In the midst of this intense discussion, I heard my grandfather mention, 'Why don't you make your prize winning phirni?'

This simple suggestion directed to my grandmother piqued my curiosity and I went on to hound her to tell me more about this 'prize winning phirni'. At first, she just brushed it aside saying my grandfather was exaggerating. But with some persistence, she finally relented, and narrated to me the story of her prize winning dish. Decades ago, my great grandfather seated in the garden with his morning tea and newspaper, stumbled upon a pamphlet attached to the last page. It announced a cooking competition being organized by the residents welfare association of the colony in our local club - a grand event inviting home chefs to book stalls, sell their culinary creations for charity, and win exciting prizes! He thought it was a splendid way to introduce my grandmother who was then a new bride to the entire community and help her make new friends in the neighborhood while helping out with a charitable cause.

Initially, my grandma was hesitant but the prospect of meeting neighbors and becoming a part of the community persuaded her. Deciding on which dish to make for the competition was the toughest part and after much deliberation and discussion with everyone in the house, it was settled that the dish was going to be an Indian dessert Phirni - a choice influenced by my grandma's notorious sweet tooth. The days leading up to the competition were a whirlwind of activity. My grandmother meticulously gathered the finest ingredients, each one a promise of perfection. Finally, the day of the competition arrived. She set up her stall with a mixture of excitement and nervousness, the aroma of cardamom and saffron wafting through the air, drawing curious onlookers.

As she served her phirni, she engaged in cheerful conversation with the neighborhood ladies and ultimately her phirni was a hit! She won the first prize of INR 1000, a sum significant in those days, but the true reward was her lifelong friends and partners-in-crime she made at the event, who have added richness to her life even in her sickness, much like the spices in her prized dessert.

Preparation time: 40 minutes
Cooking time: 30 minutes

Ingredients

150 gm rice
750 ml milk
100 ml water
2 serving spoons sugar
½ tsp green cardamom powder
3-4 strands saffron
Handful of dry fruits

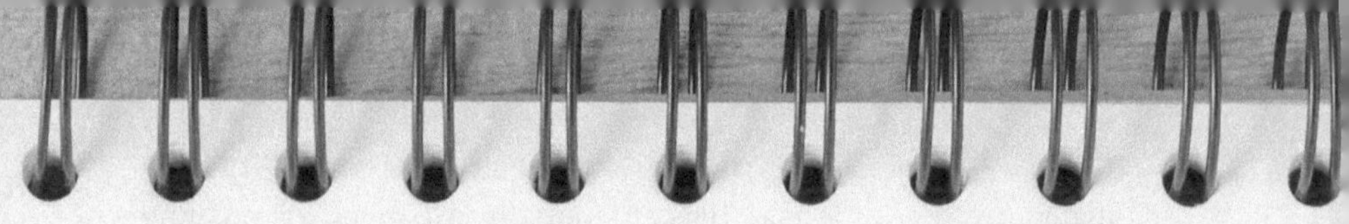

Procedure

1. Soak the rice for 30 minutes.
2. Grind them finely in a blender.
3. Boil the ground rice with a little water, cardamom powder and milk on a slow flame and let it cook for 20 minutes till it thickens.
4. Add sugar and saffron and cook for another 10 minutes till the rice is fully cooked.
5. Pour the rice pudding in earthen bowls and garnish with chopped almonds, pistachios and raisins.
6. Put it in a refrigerator for cooling for 2 hours.
7. Enjoy your phirni!

'Pani Puri'

Cultural Significance

Pani puri, widely known as golgappa in the Northern and phuchka in the Eastern parts of India, is a crispy, round, small, shell filled with a mixture of potatoes, spiced water and chutneys. Pani puri can be found everywhere in India, displaying how deeply woven it is into the country's rich culture. It is more than just a street food - it is a centuries old legacy that brings India's flavors and cultures together.

Background

Pani puri, a quintessential street food of Delhi, is a culinary delight that tantalizes the taste buds with its symphony of sweet, sour, and spicy flavors. The city's streets are dotted with hawkers, each surrounded by eager crowds - young and old alike - patiently waiting in long queues, clutching pattals (disposable bowls made of leaves), anticipating the moment when the vendor will hand them an overflowing pani puri brimming with tangy flavored water. As children, it was really enticing to watch the artful scenes of the hawker making the pani puri by carefully making a hole in the hollow ball of dough and filling it up with 2-3 sauces (chutneys) followed by masala and spicy water. It was mesmerizing to watch the vendor's hands as they moved in a dance of precision. We would watch wide-eyed as people would try to fit the entire pani puri into their mouths in one go to prevent it from bursting and spilling its contents.

Every trip to the local market was accompanied by relentless pleas to our grandma for a taste of pani puri. However, being the overprotective grandma, she wouldn't allow us, saying it was 'unhygienic' and we could fall ill as the hands of the hawkers were not clean and being on the roadside, the dust would contaminate the water.

Resourceful as always, she concocted her own recipe at home for us. Soon this became our favorite appetizer at my grandmother's home. She would sit at the dining table with a big bowl of freshly prepared pani puri and a tray filled with accompaniments. My cousins and I would circle around her, like bees hovering over a honey pot, holding out our katoris (bowls), stuffing our mouths with her special pani puris with water dripping from the sides, competing with each other as to who could eat the most. Her hands quickly replenished our finished bowls as fast as she could and you could see the smile and satisfaction on her face as she saw us gorge on her golgappas, knowing they were hygienic and safe.

It was not just the taste that made these moments special but the love and thought she poured into each pani puri that make us cherish them even today.

🕑   **Preparation time: 1 hour**

🍲   **Cooking time: 20 minutes**

Ingredients

Pani Puri

   250 gms/ 1 cup semolina

   4 tbsp lukewarm oil

   100-200 ml water

   300-400 ml of oil for frying

Filling

   2 potatoes

   100 gms chickpeas (small)

   ½ tsp black salt

   ½ tsp roasted cumin powder

   ½ tsp red chili powder

   ½ tsp chaat masala

   ½ tsp salt

   3-4 sprigs of coriander

Spicy water
  1 cup coriander
  ¼ cup mint leaves
  1 inch piece of ginger
  2 green chilis
  2 tbsp lemon juice
  ½ tsp amchoor powder (dry mango powder)
  1 tsp black salt
  1 tsp salt
  ½ tsp roasted cumin powder
  ½ tsp chaat masala
  ¼ tsp red chili powder
  3 tbsp tamarind chutney (saunth)
  ½ tsp sugar
  3 cups water
  Some raita boondi (optional)

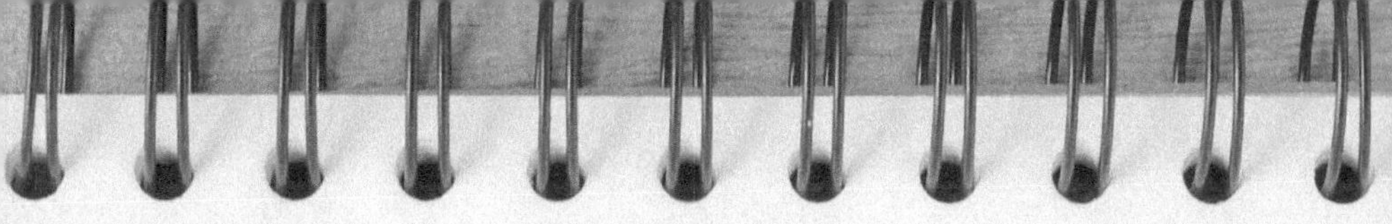

Procedure

1. Take the semolina in a bowl.
2. Add lukewarm oil to it.
3. Then add hot water.
4. Mix well with your fingers and knead for 5-7 minutes into a smooth dough.
5. Roll the dough and cut into equal size balls.
6. Flatten the balls with a rolling pin into small circular discs and deep fry them till they rise and become golden brown.
7. Drain any excess oil and transfer the puris to a plate.
8. Now prepare the filling by first boiling the potatoes and the chickpeas.
9. Once boiled, peel the potatoes and break them into small pieces with your fingers.
10. Add the boiled chickpeas and the rest of the ingredients for the filling to the potatoes and mix well. Finely chop the coriander and add that to the mixture.
11. To prepare the water, put the coriander, mint, ginger, green chili in a blender with some water and blend to make a fine paste and sieve it.
12. Add 3 cups of water and rest of the ingredients to the paste and mix well.
13. The spicy water mix is ready, transfer to a jug or big bowl and add some raita boondi. (optional)
14. Make a small hole in the panipuri, put the little filling and the spice water mix in it.
15. Serve!

'Jalebi'

Cultural Significance

Believed to have been invented in Jabalpur, India in 1889, Jalebi is a sweet treat that has captivated the hearts of many. It is made by deep-frying a batter into spiral shapes that is dip-fried in hot sugar syrup making it crunchy on the outside and soft and syrupy on the inside. This makes it a very popular sweet among all age groups in India, with many regional adaptations to its name and recipes. It's hard to resist the beautiful mix of textures and flavors created by the combination of crispy Jalebi and creamy Rabri!

Background

Nearly fifty years ago (when my grandma was twenty four), she got married to my grandfather, a man who was her complete opposite: a modern westernized Indian Punjabi boy who had studied abroad. To her total dismay, he did not have a palate for Indian snacks and desserts. For any guests visiting her home, they would usually be treated to crispy samosas (a savory pastry filled with spicy potatoes), salted snacks, and jalebis (a syrup-soaked spiral dessert). My grandmother would guzzle these Jalebis up in a matter of a few milliseconds without considering the high sugar content. However, my grandfather really struggled to pretend to enjoy these snacks made specially for the son in law of the house - him!

On Dussehra - the day after Navratras - it was a tradition to visit my grandma's childhood home and see the auspicious burning of the effigy of Ravana (signifying the victory of good over evil). On this special occasion, the halwai (confectioner) near her house used to make a colossal round jaleb, so large that it couldn't even fit in a child's hands.

It was ceremoniously cut like a birthday cake, with the youngest child given the honor of wielding the knife while everyone else gathered around in eager anticipation. Once the effigy of the Ravana being burnt was seen from the window, everyone would descend upon the jalebi, tearing into it with delight.

This brought immense joy and content to everyone. My grandmother, in particular, cherishes these moments, where tradition, family, and the irresistible allure of sugary treats came together in perfect harmony. Today even though we no longer get to visit her childhood home, my grandmother continues to treat us to her mouth-watering jalebis, which my grandfather too honestly enjoys!

A note from my grandma

Since jalebi was my favorite sweet as a child, I was affectionately nicknamed Baby rhyming with Jalebi. Everytime I entered my childhood home, the house would echo with 'O Jalebi Baby is here!'. To this day, I love jalebis but due to my sickness, I am not allowed to have sugar. Even a small piece of it brings me joy now. I hope to get well soon so I can make jalebis for everyone again, watch their mouths water in anticipation and indulge in the sumptuous sweet myself!

🕐 **Preparation time: 15 minutes**
🍲 **Cooking time: 25 minutes**

Ingredients

Syrup
  1 cup water
  1 cup sugar
  2-3 sprigs of saffron

Jalebi mix
  1 cup flour
  1 cup water
  1 tsp baking powder
  Ghee/oil
  Orange food coloring

Procedure

1. Mix the water, sugar and saffron. Boil till it becomes sticky and slightly thick.
2. Remove from fire and keep aside (this is the syrup mix).
3. Mix flour, water, one spoon of ghee, baking powder and a pinch of food coloring till the batter is consistent.
4. Pour a bit of this batter in a funnel made of a plastic bag with one of the tips cut.
5. Heat the oil/ghee for a couple minutes till it gets hot.
6. Swirl the batter from top into the oil into spiral shapes.
7. Fry till they turn goldenish-brown.
8. Take them out and dip them in the syrup for 2-3 minutes.
9. Serve!

'Shami Kebab'

Cultural Significance

Shami kebabs are delicious, soft patties made from meat and a variety of spices. Originating in the historic city of Lucknow in Uttar Pradesh, the heart of the Mughal Empire, shami kebabs are said to have been invented by a talented chef serving a great Nawab who had lost all his teeth. The chef created shami kebabs, a dish so soft that it could be savored even by the toothless.

Background

As a young girl, my grandmother's first visit to Lucknow, also known as the "City of Nawabs", was to attend the wedding of my great grandmother's friend's daughter. Both my great grandmother and her friend had been inseparable since their childhood days in Lahore, Pakistan. While my great grandmother stayed in Delhi, her friend settled with her family in Lucknow post partition. The wedding of her friend's daughter was a highly anticipated event that my grandmother could not miss. On the way from the railway station to the wedding venue, my grandmother witnessed the ancient architectural wonders of the city such as the majestic Bara and Chhota Imambara and the iconic Rumi Darwaza. The exuberant scenes of the vibrant bazaars adorned with clothes, jewelry, shoes and numerous stalls selling tantalizing kebabs and biryani were a sight to behold. It was at that moment that she decided a visit to one of these bustling bazaars was a must during her trip.

Soon after the wedding festivities, my grandmother and her friends slipped away to a nearby market renowned for its kebab shops. My grandma was awestruck by the sheer number of shami kebab, tunday kebab and tandoor shops lining the bustling streets. The electrifying atmosphere and the enticing aromas were a feast for the senses, but nothing prepared her for the moment she took her first bite of a shami kebab. The flavors were so exquisite that she was immediately captivated. Desperately trying to uncover the culinary secrets behind the delectable shami kebab, my grandma engaged in a 'discussion' with the local dhaba cook. The cook, most likely amused, ultimately relented and shared his recipe, though my grandma always suspected he did not reveal a few secret ingredients. But this gave my grandma an opportunity to experiment and concoct her own version of the sumptuous shami kebab she tried in the bustling streets of lucknow. Her relentless pursuit of recreating that unforgettable taste not only satisfied her own cravings but also created a legacy of culinary delight for our family.

🕑 **Preparation time: 20 minutes**

🍲 **Cooking time: 1 hour**

Ingredients

250 gm minced meat (lamb)

200 gm chana dal

1 big onion finely chopped

1 pod garlic

2 small cinnamon sticks

2 cloves

5 whole black peppers

4 green cardamoms

½ tsp red chilli powder

Salt to taste

2 tbsp oil

1 cup water

1 slice bread

25 gm fresh coriander leaves

2 green chilli

Oil

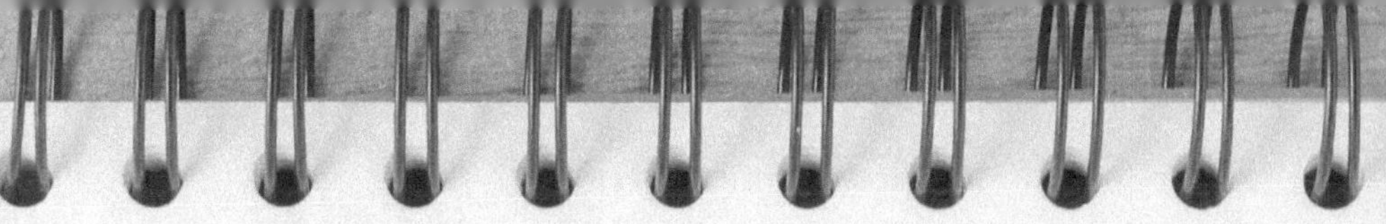

Procedure

1. Soak the chana dal for 10 minutes.
2. Put oil in a pan.
3. Add all the spices in the pan.
4. Add chopped garlic and onion in the pan till slightly brown.
5. Add minced meat and cook on medium flame for 10 minutes till the water dries and the meat turns slightly brownish in color.
6. Add the soaked chana dal, salt and red chilli powder and cook together for 15 more minutes.
7. Add water and pressure cook it on medium flame for 10 minutes (5 whistles).
8. Take out the mixture and separate the whole spices.
9. Cool the mixture.
10. Grind the mixture in a blender along with fresh coriander leaves, green chilli and 1 slice of bread.
11. Take the mixture out and make it into flat, round patties.
12. Put the mixture in the refrigerator for 1 hour.
13. Shallow fry these with some heated oil in a pan.
14. Enjoy with some pickled onions and green chutney!

'Chocolate Halwa'

Cultural Significance

The first appearance of 'Halwa' was showcased in the 13th century Arabic text 'Kitab-al-Tabikh' which featured eight varieties of this delightful confection along with their recipes. The word 'halwa' is derived from the word 'hulw' which means sweet. Remarkably, it can remain unspoilt for months without adding any preservatives and refrigeration. It was mainly made of date paste and milk. In India, there is a halwa for almost every occasion!

Background

In our household, halwa is an indispensable part of festivals, special occasions such as birthdays, anniversaries and auspicious events where after the Puja (spiritual ceremony where prayers are made to deities), it is first offered to God and then distributed as prasad to everyone present. This ritual underscores the significance of Halwa in our cultural and religious practices. It is also one of the first dishes that a new bride prepares as one of her first culinary contributions upon entering her new home.

My grandmother, the quintessential matriarch of our family, faithfully upholds these traditions. On every birthday or festive occasion, the first sign of celebration in the morning is the enticing aroma of halwa wafting in the kitchen.

As a child, I was a notoriously fussy eater, particularly disinterested in Indian sweets and would often avoid eating halwa which would greatly upset the elders of the house as they would force me to take some which I reluctantly would. Understanding this lack of enthusiasm and my profound fondness for chocolates, my grandmother being as resourceful and inventive as she is, decided to come to my rescue and lo and behold, devised her famous recipe of chocolate halwa, which integrated my favorite dessert - chocolate with the traditional Indian sweet - halwa making it wholesome and tasty!

Today, chocolate halwa has become a beloved staple in our celebrations. On birthday mornings, the anticipation of this small treat brings the entire family together, each of us eager to enjoy the delicious dish crafted by my grandmother's loving hands. Her innovative approach has not only made Halwa more appealing to me but has also created a new tradition that everyone in our family cherishes.

🕐 **Preparation time: 10 minutes**
🍲 **Cooking time: 30 minutes**

Ingredients

200 gm semolina

50 gm besan (gram flour)

100 gm desi ghee

400 ml of milk

2 eggs

2 tbsp cocoa powder

150 gm white sugar

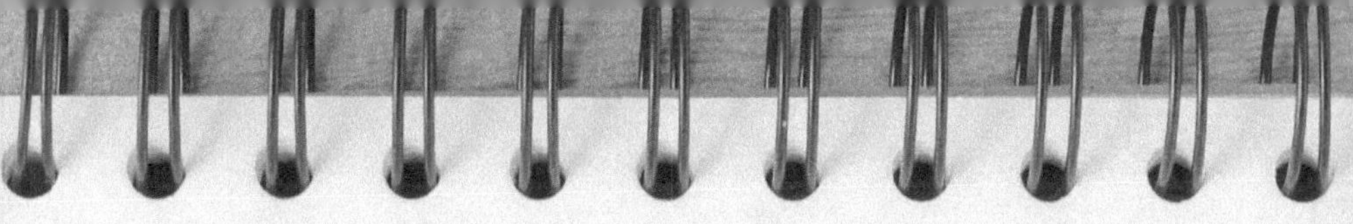

Procedure

1. Heat a pan and put the desi ghee in it. Once hot, add semolina and slightly roast it.
2. Then add the gram flour and continue roasting till it is golden brown.
3. Beat two eggs, milk, cocoa powder and the sugar together in a bowl. Whisk nicely till all ingredients are mixed thoroughly.
4. Reduce the flame and add the milk mixture to the semolina and gram flour in the pan and stir continuously.
5. Let it cook for 15 minutes till the semolina turns soft and the mixture thickens
6. Pour into a bowl.
7. Bon appetit!

'Kabuli Pulao'

Cultural Significance

A staple at any Afghan gathering, 'Kabuli Pao' is renowned for its rich, comforting flavor and blend of spices known as masala. It normally features steamed rice mixed with marinated lamb meat. It is generously adorned with lots of dry fruits - dried raisins, almonds, dried apricots - and vegetables like carrots. It usually forms the centerpiece of any meal, with other dishes placed around it. Each bite is an explosion of flavors and texture: the soft marinated meat, delightful interplay between the dry fruits and vegetables, and the aromatic spices. Anyone who tastes it is bound to be licking their fingers till not a speck of rice is left!

Background

Originally from the rugged terrains of Afghanistan, the recipe of the infamous 'Kabuli Pulao' reached Pakistan (where my great grandparents grew up) through ancient trade routes. In the aftermath of the 1947 partition, amidst absolute chaos and disarray, the treasured recipe of their ancestral home, an aromatic reminder of the life they had left behind, traveled with them to their new homeland. Traditionally, it has meat in it but being the quintessential pious Indian family and thus strict vegetarians, my great grandmother meticulously modified it to a vegetarian delight through relentless experimentation using locally made easily available ingredients.

Having seven children, my great grandmother always found the kitchen a battlefield of sorts, where pleasing every palate was a Herculean task. However, 'Kabuli Pulao' was an easy one pot dish which was relished by all her children and quelled any dinnertime dissent. The exotic aroma of spices mingling with rich desi ghee would fill the house, promising everyone a comforting meal.

As tradition would have it, the recipe was then passed down as a proud family heirloom to my grandmother. Even though my grandfather is now restrained by dietary restrictions due to his ailments, there was a time when he would salivate at the mere thought of Kabuli Pao being made in the house: still not more than my mother and her brother though! As children, it was their favorite kind of dish to savor and ranked even ahead of the sumptuous chicken and mutton biryanis (which is a lot to say for a couple of Punjabi teenagers!).

Being a fitness enthusiast myself, it remains a guilty pleasure to this day. The dish, with its rich flavors and storied past, serves as a bridge connecting my family's past to its present, a testament to the culinary legacy and heritage of our ancestors.

🕗 **Preparation time: 1hour**
🍲 **Cooking time: 30 minutes**

Ingredients

300 gms basmati rice

3 onions

2 slices of white bread

2 tomatoes

1 tbsp chana masala

100 gms kabuli chana (Chickpeas)

1 tsp red chili powder

2 tsp salt

100 gms desi ghee

1 carrot (thinly sliced)

3-4 tindas (Indian round gourd - sliced)

200 ml milk

1 lemon

10-15 raisins

2-3 dried apricots (chopped)

8-10 almonds (sliced)

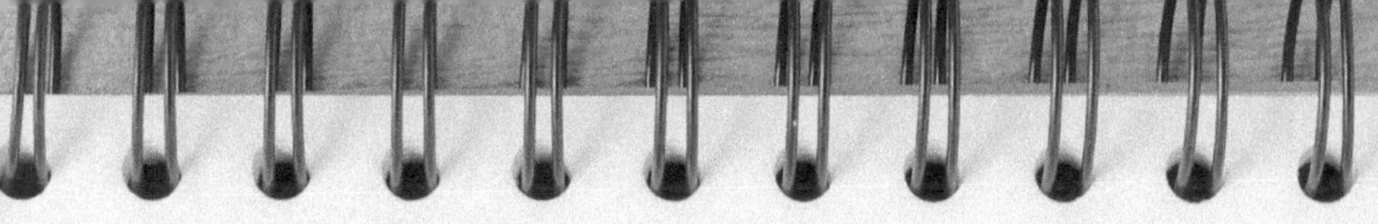

Procedure

1. Soak basmati rice in water for 30 mins.
2. Boil it with a pinch of salt.
3. Once boiled, keep aside.
4. Slice red onions and fry the onions in desi ghee in a pan.
5. Put cut tomatoes and dried apricots in the pan. Cook till they soften.
6. Put a little red chili and a pinch of salt in this mixture.
7. Cut square pieces of bread and slightly fry them.
8. In another pan, take half the cooked mix of tomato and onion.
9. Put some chana masala and add the boiled kabuli chanas in it.
10. Keep aside.
11. Pan fry the sliced carrots and the tindas.
12. Take 1 glass of slightly warm milk and juice of 1 lemon.
13. Take a round glass bowl so that one can see the layers.
14. Put slightly melted ghee in it.
15. Put 2 inches of boiled rice and press it with a spatula.
16. Then put a layer of kabuli chana.
17. Again put 1 tbsp of desi ghee.
18. Layer the tomato onion mixture along with the fried bread pieces and fried Indian round gourd (tinda)
19. Layer white rice.
20. Put curdled milk on top.
21. Put a very thin layer of boiled rice, sprinkle with fried carrot and dry fruits (sweet raisins and almonds).
22. Cover for 10 mins.
23. Serve!

'Walnuts and Dates Cake'

Background

It was the year 1975, and shortly after her marriage, my grandmother had gone to visit her elder sister. On entering her sister's house, she was intoxicated by the bewitching aroma of a cake. This drove her curiosity wild as she bombarded her sister with a multitude of questions about the type of cake, flavor and ingredients. However, to my grandmother's absolute dismay, even her sister was oblivious about the recipe of the cake being baked in the oven. The cake had apparently been conjured by my grandmother's sister's mother in law who withheld all her recipes in a secret diary. The 'walnuts and dates cake' was one of her 'signature secret recipes' which everyone imagined only she herself would hold the key to until she was no more.

Undeterred, my grandmother utilized the five kilometers short distance between their houses to the fullest as she would seize every opportunity to visit and spend time with her. One day, my grandmother baked a simple chocolate cake for her. This small act of kindness unlocked the key to the old woman's heart and recipe diary! She went into her room, unlocked a drawer and retrieved a yellowed, half-torn diary titled "My Recipes," its pages worn with age and filled with culinary secrets. My grandma was overwhelmed with ecstasy, having finally discovered the coveted secret diary!

One random day in peak lockdown 2020, when everyone seemed to have become professional chefs and homebound bakers, my grandmother invited me over for dinner and dessert. Little did I know I was about to taste the most consummate walnuts and dates cake ever! This marked the beginning of our baking journey: I remember spending innumerable hours with her in the kitchen, perching on a small stool barely reaching over her shoulder, but still determined to absorb every minute detail of the baking process of the exquisite cake like how she would crush the dates and prepare the batter. Infact, one of my fondest memories with her include laughing together for time on end as I would mimic her exact motion while making the cake and persistently inquire about the measurements of each ingredient.

The walnuts and dates cake recipe is thus a very treasured recipe in my heart as it not only was the most delectable treat, but the combination of walnuts and dates also represented the strong bond between my grandmother and me, incomplete without the other.

🕗 **Preparation time: 20 minutes**
🍲 **Cooking time: 40 minutes**

Ingredients

1 cup walnuts chopped
1 cup seedless dates chopped
1 cup sugar
1.5 cup flour
1 cup boiling water
1 egg
1 spoon baking powder
1 spoon baking soda
Pinch of salt

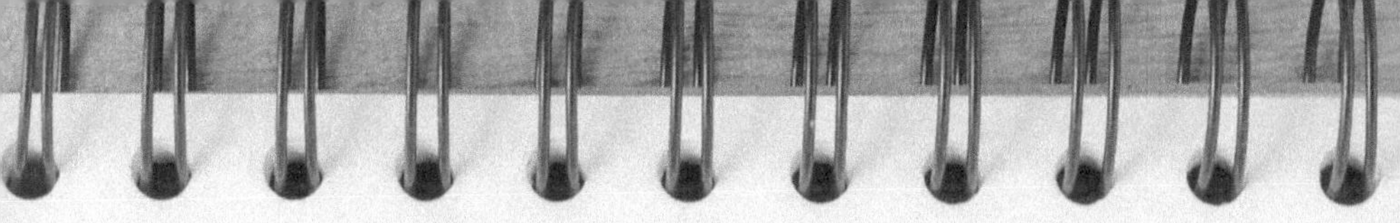

Procedure

1. Preheat the oven to 180 degrees.
2. Mix walnuts, dates and sugar in boiling water in a cup and beat it up.
3. Add baking powder and baking soda (it should become frothy at this time).
4. Mix it again.
5. Sieve the flour and keep transferring 1 spoon of the flour repeatedly in the mixture.
6. Beat the egg and mix it in the same batter.
7. Add **just** a pinch of salt.
8. Grease the baking dish with oil and sprinkle white flour on it.
9. Pour the batter in the dish and insert in the oven at 180 degrees for 40 minutes.
10. Check with a fork or toothpick whether it is fully cooked.
11. Serve!

Nani's pro tip:

- Put the dates with a little water in a food processor, coarsely grind, then mix together with the sugar and chopped walnuts.
- Add chilled cream to the cake when serving for the most exquisite taste!

A snap from my grandma's diary!

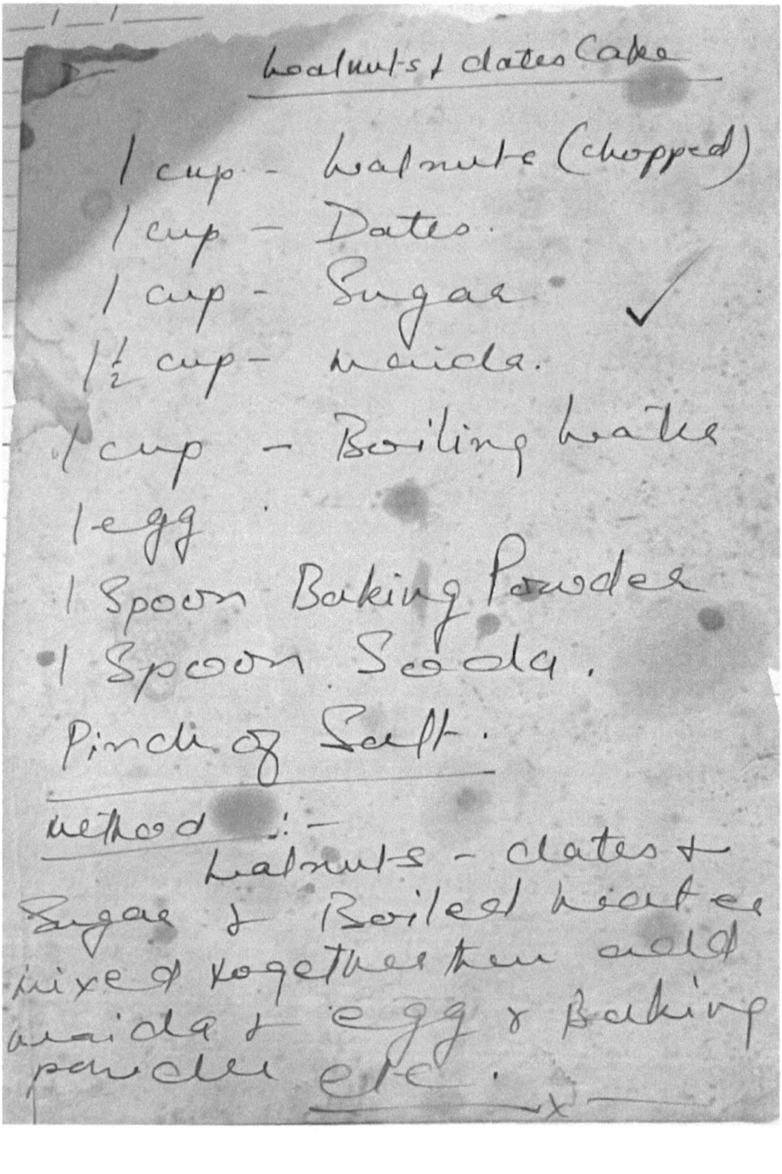

Walnuts & dates Cake

1 cup - Walnuts (chopped)
1 cup - Dates.
1 cup - Sugar ✓
1½ cup - maida.
1 cup - Boiling water
1 egg.
1 Spoon Baking Powder
1 Spoon Soda.
Pinch of Salt.

Method :-

Walnuts - dates & Sugar & Boiled water mixed together then add maida & egg & Baking powder etc.

—x—

'Sindhi Kadhi'

Cultural Significance

Sindhi cuisine became a significant part of Indian culinary traditions with the migration of the Sindhi Hindus from Pakistan during the partition in 1947. Sindhi kadhi is a tangy concoction of gram flour, tomatoes and tamarind, which is packed with nutrients in addition to being delicious. It is a special dish prepared on one of the significant Sindhi Hindu festivals of 'Teejri'. On this day, Sindhi women keep a fast throughout the day for the wellbeing of their husbands and break it in the evening only after seeing the stars in the sky. After breaking their fast, they enjoy a sumptuous meal of Sindhi Kadhi and rice with their families as it is believed to bring good health and fortune to the family. In fact, Sindhis even have a ceremony called 'Kadhi Chawal' a day before a wedding, where Sindhi Kadhi and rice are made and first served to Brahmins, followed by the guests. Today, Sindhi cuisine has gained popularity globally, spreading joy and contentment to one and all.

Background

As I sat on the terrace with my grandmother on a sunny winter afternoon, enjoying a warm bowl of sindhi kadhi and rice she had prepared specially for me, I could see her drift into a nostalgic reverie. A moment later, I found her face radiating with a big smile as she gently caressed my hair and said, "You know Ameya, eating kadhi chawal in your terrace garden has reminded me of some of my favorite childhood memories. When I was your age, we lived on the University campus. The best part was that the houses there had huge gardens with lush green grass and tall trees. Our neighbor was a Sindhi lady, Mrs. Atwani, who had four children. She was good friends with your great-grandmother, and every evening, my brother and I, along with the neighborhood boys, would go to her house to play cricket. Even though I was the only girl, I enjoyed myself immensely - probably because I loved to bat but always found an excuse to miss fielding - much to the boys' resentment!"

She continued, "I remember how your great-grandfather would bring piping hot samosas and jalebis for all of us on his way from work, and after hours of playing, we would pounce on the food, gobbling it down in what seemed like less than a minute. I guess this probably made up for my cheating and ensured my place in the team. In the winters, Mrs. Atwani's grand potluck picnic in her garden was the most awaited ritual. We would carry the rice and she would make her famous Sindhi Kadhi. After all the fun and games, we would sit on the daris(mats) in the garden and she would serve us some of the finest Sindhi delicacies. Eating her sumptuous Sindhi Kadhi with rice was heavenly, and even after several helpings, I could still make space for more. When we moved to our own house after a few years, the one thing I knew I would miss the most was Mrs. Atwani's Sindhi Kadhi. To my delight, she shared her recipe with your great-grandmother, who then passed it on to me. And today, that's how you are enjoying this finger licking kadhi!"

I knew then, if I wanted to continue to enjoy some of these recipes passed down from generations, I had to spend some more time in the kitchen with my grandmother!

🕐 **Preparation time: 30 minutes**
🍲 **Cooking time: 30 minutes**

Ingredients

½ medium sized brinjal

100 gms small ladyfingers

2 small potatoes

½ medium sized cauliflower

½ kg ripe tomatoes

2 tbsp ghee

1 tbsp oil
1 tsp methra (fenugreek seeds)
½ tsp red chili powder
Pinch of hing (asafoetida)
4 tbsp gram flour
8-10 curry leaves
¼ tsp sugar
Salt to taste

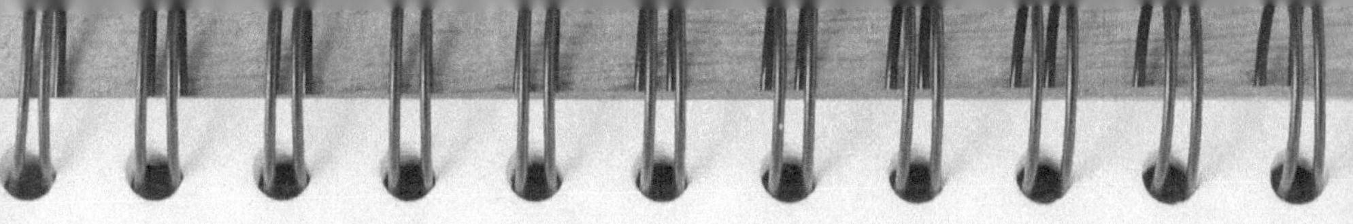

Procedure

1. Dice the brinjal into medium size pieces and slightly slit the ladyfingers after removing their cap.
2. Heat 1 tbsp of oil in a pan and saute the ladyfingers and brinjal for 7-8 minutes. Drain and put aside.
3. Slice the potatoes and cauliflower and boil them for 15-20 minutes in some water till they are tender.
4. Boil the tomatoes and peel them. Blend to make a puree.
5. Take a kadai and add the ghee and heat it. Once hot, add hing, methra and curry leaves.
6. Add the gram flour and roast it till it becomes golden brown. Turn off the flame and add the tomato puree and 1 cup of water. Stir continuously so that there are no lumps.
7. Put the flame on again and add the salt, red chili powder and the boiled vegetables and let it simmer till the kadhi thickens.
8. If it tastes sour add a little sugar.
9. Serve the curry with steamed rice.

'Lemon Drizzle Cake'

Background

Let me take you back to the year 2013 when my grandmother hosted David Cameron, the British Prime Minister and around 20 representatives from the House of Lords to the institute she was the principal of. One of these dignitaries, absolutely impressed by my grandmother's candidness and effervescent charm, graciously invited her to visit the House of Lords in London. Overjoyed to hear this news, my grandmother spent the next few days packing her finest sarees and selecting thoughtful gifts. However, the high cost of staying at a hotel near the House of Lords posed a significant obstacle. Thus, my grandmother decided to rather travel to Basingstoke to stay with her close friend, Shobhana, and what better day to visit her than Shobhana's husband's birthday?

Upon her arrival, my grandmother was greeted by the typical London rainy and dreary weather. Despite the dismal weather, the fresh dew drops fallen on the leaves in Shobhana's lush green garden filled with flowers in full bloom along with the earthy rainy scent of her vegetable garden seemed delightful, as compared to the stifling humidity of Delhi rains. Their plans to explore London and check items off the long shopping list she had meticulously made were quickly thwarted by the relentless downpour. That's when Shobhana came up with an ingenious plan: "Indu, why not bake something together? How about..?" My grandmother eagerly waiting to hear her complete her sentence, leaned in. 'Lemon Drizzle Cake!' Shobhana exclaimed. They spent the next couple of hours collecting all required ingredients, only to discover there were no lemons to be found!

Just then, they looked outside the glass window to the garden where there were a handful of fresh strawberries, lemons and grapes growing! 'Truly homemade!' exclaimed Shobhana. What began as a friendly baking session led to a competitive bake off, with Shobhana's expertise in the making of the lemon drizzle cake ultimately securing her the win.

That evening, when Shobhana's husband came back, the first words out of his mouth were, 'Wow! What's that I smell?" Both my grandmother and Shobhana emerged from the kitchen, proudly holding up their cake, singing 'Happy birthday!'. He took his first bite, exclaiming 'Mhm! That is heavenly!'

Despite the rain, the day was filled with warmth, laughter, spirited competition and a zeal for cooking culminating in a memorable celebration and sweet success!

🕗 **Preparation time: 15 minutes**
🍲 **Cooking time: 30 minutes**

Ingredients

Cake

   125 gm butter/margarine

   125 gm sugar

   2 large eggs

   Zest of 1 lemon

   175 gm self-raising flour

   Pinch of salt

   4 tbsp milk

Drizzle

   2 tsp icing sugar

   2 tsp lemon juice

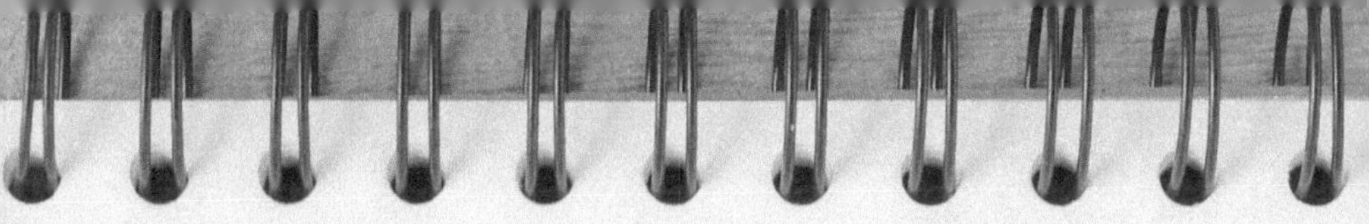

Procedure

1. Preheat the oven to 180 degrees.
2. Beat eggs.
3. Take a bowl, mix eggs, butter, lemon, sugar, and milk.
4. Mix salt in the flour and sieve.
5. Mix both flour and egg, butter mixture together.
6. Grease the baking dish.
7. Pour mixed batter in a baking dish.
8. Place the baking dish in the oven and let it bake for 30 minutes.
9. Now for the lemon drizzle, mix the icing sugar and lemon juice.
10. Warm in the microwave.
11. After checking that the cake is fully baked, pour drizzle on top.
12. Bon appetit!

A snap from my grandma's diary!

Lemon Drizzel Cake
Tried & good
Shobhana's Recipe
U.K
125 gm Butter (margarine)
175 gm Sugar
2 Large Eggs
Zest of one lemon peel of one lemon (lemon Rind)
175 gm self raising flour
(or put baking powder)
Pinch of Salt
— Mix Butter & Sugar. — Eggs.
= mix salt in flour तैयार र
— put Eggs र Beal.
zivel र flour
— Tin सो grease —
→ 4 tablespoons of Milk.
Temp. 180° pre heated oven
उतारने से
— Icing Sugar र lemon juice
dissolve warm it up
in the micro wave
2 tspn Sugar र 2 tspons आटा उंट
once the cake comes out
poke it with a skewer

'Roganjosh and Al-Roganjosh'

Cultural Significance

Kashmiri cuisine is very versatile and resplendent with rich aromatic flavors and a unique blend of spices and cooking techniques. It is an amalgamation of Central Asian, Persian and North Indian culinary traditions which represents the religious as well as the socio-cultural heritage of the region. Its history can be traced back to the fifteenth century when Timur, a ruler from Central Asia, invaded India and the descendents of the cooks (the Wazas) that had migrated to India during the invasion introduced the Wazwan cuisine in the region.

One of its most distinct features is how the same food can be cooked in different ways based on the community preparing it. The Kashmiri Pandits use no onions, garlic or tomatoes in their cooking, relying primarily on spice and curd, while Kashmiri Muslims use the base vegetables for preparation of the curry. The method of slow cooking, combined with roasting or deep frying depending on the dish, is central to the outcome. Though often thought to consist mostly of non-vegetarian dishes, Kashmiri cuisine is rich in both vegetarian and non-vegetarian foods, with the same recipe often used to cook a non-vegetarian and a vegetarian dish. An example would be meat cooked as yakhni and bottle gourd as yakhni, or meat as rogan josh and pumpkin as rogan josh.

Background

Kashmir, with its alluring beauty and picture perfect landscapes, is often called as 'Paradise on Earth' or ' Jannat-e-Jahan'. Just like its stunning natural beauty, the rich Kashmiri Wazwan cuisine is heavenly and boasts of several delectable dishes. Despite having traveled all over the world, Kashmir remains on my grandparents' bucket list, a destination they've yet to visit despite several plans.

I would often see my grandmother watching videos of people traveling to Kashmir, trying to soak in its beauty virtually and exploring Kashmiri recipes on YouTube. One day, when I visited my grandmother after school, I found her filled with excitement. She exclaimed, "Guess what, Ameya? I have been invited for a special dinner! Help me select my saree."

I wondered, "Special dinner, Nani?"

She then explained, "A colleague of mine from Kashmir has invited your grandfather and me to her house for a Kashmiri Wazwan meal. She's a wonderful cook, and I can't wait to taste some authentic Kashmiri delicacies."

The next day, when I returned from school, I found my grandmother sitting on the dining table with a bowl of Mutton Roganjosh, eagerly waiting for me to taste it. As I sat with her to eat my lunch, she rambled on about how fantastic the dinner was, the delightful conversations they had surrounding Kashmir, and how the experience strengthened her resolve to visit Kashmir sooner rather than later. She recounted how the Kashmiri food exceeded her expectations, and she couldn't resist asking her colleague to pack some for me to taste. She went on, "I had the most delicious Roganjosh, Yakhni Pulao, Dum Aloo, Goshtaba and Nadru Yakhni. Not only me, even your grandfather was licking his fingers and complimenting the food." (That definitely meant something coming from my grandfather who is quite the food critic and not easily pleased).

As I took a spoonful of the rogan josh, it melted in my mouth, delivering such a flavorful punch. It proved to be a true testament of all that my grandmother was proclaiming. As I finished my lunch, I could see my grandmother searching frantically in her bag. She pulled out a folded piece of paper and as she opened it with a beaming smile, she said, "You'll never guess what I got, Ameya! It's the recipe for the mouthwatering mutton rogan josh you just ate. My colleague was kind enough to share it with me." Just then I knew, we had our work cut out for the next few days till we perfected the perfect recipe!

⊗ **Preparation time: 10 minutes**

🫕 **Cooking time: 1 hour**

Ingredients for both

500 gms of Meat **(for Roganjosh)**/pumpkin **(for Al-Roganjosh)**

1 tbsp mustard oil

4-6 cloves

3-4 green cardamom

2-3 big cardamom

1 Tej pata (bay leaf) - optional

2 tsp powdered red chilli (for color and heat - can also be increased for your taste)

1 tsp of jeera (cumin)

1 tsp of hing (asafoetida)

4 heaped tsp of powdered saunf (fennel)

1 tsp of sonth (powdered ginger)

1 tsp of powdered garam masala

100 gms of curd

100ml water

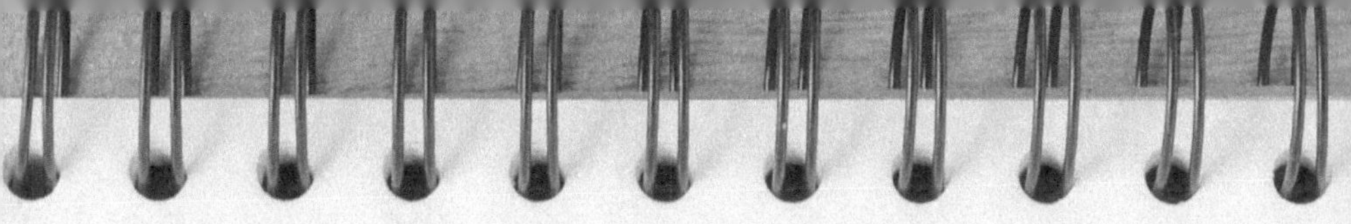

Procedure for Mutton Roganjosh

1. In your pressure cooker put the oil and heat till it smokes.
2. Turn down heat and add the hing, jeera, whole garam masala (bash it a bit), red chili powder and salt as per your taste.
3. Stir quickly so the chili does not burn and add the mutton.
4. Stir and slow fry the mutton till it begins to stop looking raw.
5. Add the saunf and the sonth and keep stirring and frying.
6. When masala gets a bit sticky add 100 ml of water.
7. Optional : Add tej patta
8. Let the mutton cook and the masala get dry and sticky.
9. When this happens add the curd and powdered garam masala. Stir and let the mutton and masala cook till it thickens and oil begins to form a layer on top.
10. Now add some water as needed for pressure cooking.
11. One big whistle and two on sim are good.
12. Once you open the cooker, allow the curry to boil to a thick consistency.
13. Enjoy with bread or rice or roti!

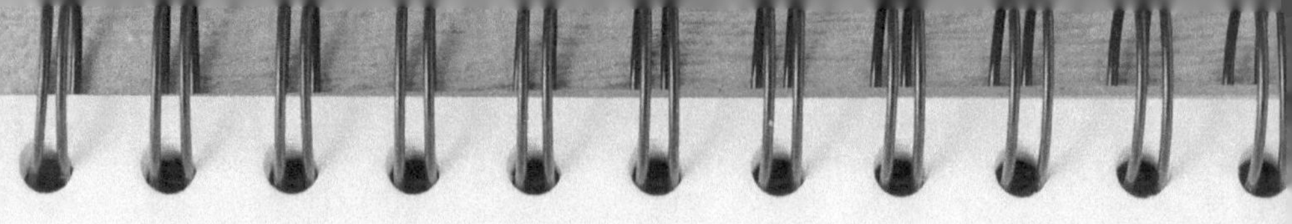

Procedure for Al-Roganjosh

1. Cut your pumpkin into large 2- 3 inch pieces without the peel.
2. Poke them all over with a fork or knife.
3. Place oil in a pressure cooker.
4. Once oil begins to smoke, put in the pumpkin and let it fry lightly and redden.
5. When this happens, add the Jeera, whole garam masala (grind it a bit), Red chili powder, Salt as per your taste, fennel powder and ginger powder.
6. Stir so the chilli doesn't burn.
7. After about 2 minutes of stirring add the curd and stir so it doesn't curdle.
8. Keep stirring till all masalas get a little sticky.
9. Add a cup of water and give it one whistle.
10. Once you open the pressure cooker, thicken gravy as per choice and sprinkle powdered garam masala.
11. Enjoy with rice!

Note: Optional

You can add some whole green chillies to the pumpkin when you pressure cooker it.

'Apple Pie'

Background

Come winters and I am greeted with the scent of ripe apples, cinnamon and buttery crust each time I visit my grandmother's home for dinner. Hot apple pie with chilled vanilla ice cream- a dessert combination that has become a cherished family favorite. I can see her face beaming with pride as she takes the perfect pie out of the oven and serves us perfectly cut pieces with a scoop of ice cream each.

One day after gulping my second helping, I couldn't help but ask, "Nani, where did you learn how to make such a delicious apple pie?" I could see her smiling as she recalled, "You know Ameya, it was the first recipe that I learnt at my very first cooking class. There was this lady in our neighborhood who was known for her English desserts. Your grandfather really enjoyed them and we would often order from her since we only made Indian sweets at home back then. One day, my friend excitedly told me about some dessert cooking classes and suggested we join them for fun. As luck would have it, the classes were being conducted by the very same lady from whom we used to order. I pounced on the opportunity and we joined the classes. It was the most enjoyable experience, learning with friends while cooking and tasting some amazing desserts. And guess who was happier than me? Your grandfather, because now he didn't have to order his favorite dessert from outside anymore!"

She recounted how my grandfather, who hated grocery shopping, would be more than happy to contribute to the beginning of the apple pie baking process and bring home massive baskets of fresh, organic apples from the local 'mandi' to ensure his apple pie tasted flawless. Instead of following the traditional recipe, my grandmother added her own unique twist: apple pie baked with a hint of spices like nutmeg and cinnamon. Her years of practice, dedication, and love for cooking, combined with her creative flair, have led to all of us savoring each bite, appreciating the care and delicious flavor behind it. Her apple pie truly embodies the saying, "Practice makes perfect."

⊘ **Preparation time: 2 hours**
Cooking time: 30 minutes

Ingredients

Crust
  1.5 medium sized cups flour
  100 gms butter frozen
  5 tbsp Chilled water
  ½ tsp baking powder

Filling
  500 gms apples finely chopped
  100 gm Sugar
  ½ tsp Cinnamon powder
  Pinch of nutmeg
  ½ tsp Lemon juice
  1 tsp Milk

Procedure

1. Sieve the flour in a bowl along with the baking powder, peel thin slices of frozen butter with a peeler and add to the flour.
2. With your fingers, mix the butter and flour till it becomes fine yet grainy.
3. Add 5 tbsp chilled water slowly and bind the flour mixture roughly into the shape of a ball, it does not have to be kneaded nor does it have to be smooth.
4. Wrap the dough in a thin moist cloth and let it rest in the refrigerator for 1-2 hours.
5. Prepare the apple filling by cooking the chopped apples and sugar in a pan for 20 minutes.
6. Add the cinnamon powder and nutmeg powder while it is cooking and the lemon juice when it's almost done.
7. Cool the filling.
8. Take the dough out and with the cloth, press it a little from the top to flatten it slightly.
9. Then cut the dough ball with a sharp knife: 1/4th for the cover of the pie and 3/4ths for the base.
10. Wrap the 3/4th dough in a cling wrap and flatten it with a rolling pin to make the base of the pie.
11. Wrap the 1/4th dough in a cling wrap and flatten it with a rolling pin to make the cover of the pie.
12. Remove the cling wrap, grease the baking dish with a little butter and fit the base in a baking dish covering its sides as well.
13. Fill it with the apple mixture, put the cover on top and seal it by pinching the edges.

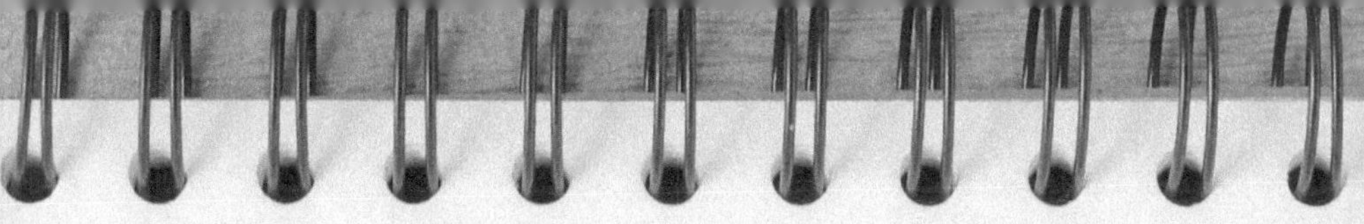

14. Sprinkle some sugar on top of the cover and slightly brush it with some milk.
15. Preheat the oven to 180 degrees.
16. Make some holes in the cover with a fork and bake it in the oven at 180 degrees for 30 minutes.

Nani's pro tip

Do not ever knead the dough for the crust, just lightly mix with the fingertips to make fine grains so that the crust is light and airy!

'Mango Kulfi'

Cultural Significance

Mangoes, scientifically known as 'Mangifera Indica', originated in India nearly four thousand years ago and are the 'National Fruit' of India. In ancient times, mangoes were referred to as 'Amra-Phal' and have even been mentioned in the Hindu scriptures namely the Upanishads and the Puranas. Mangoes are an inherent part of Indian culture, be it in religion, art, cuisine or literature. The different varieties of mangoes grown in various regions of India are known by distinct names that reflect the local people, language, and culture. To name a few, we have Alphonso, Ratnagiri, Devgad (Maharashtra), Kesar, Vanraj (Gujarat), Safeda (Andhra Pradesh), Totapuri (Karnataka) and Dusheri, Langda, Chaunsa (Uttar Pradesh).

The history of kulfi can be traced back to the sixteenth century Mughal era, deriving its name from 'qulfi', a Persian word meaning 'a covered cup'. Often referred to as the 'traditional ice cream' of India, it is a dense, creamy concoction of milk and sugar prepared using a slow cooking technique. Over time, various flavors have evolved from the classic pistachio and saffron (kesar kulfi) to seasonal varieties such as pomegranate, falsa, and mango, as well as modern fusion flavors like rose, paan, and chocolate. For me, mango being my favorite fruit and Kulfi my favorite Indian dessert, mango kulfi is a match made in heaven!

Background

It's summertime! It's mango time! You can tell that summer has begun when you see the streets lined with vendors and their carts laden with piles of brightly coloured mangoes in shades of yellow, orange, green. An invisible string of luscious aroma pulls you towards them, making it nearly impossible to resist. Summer vacations meant a full house at my grandmother's home with all cousins, uncles and aunts looking to relax and spend some quality family time together, though it was the busiest time for my grandmother who was preparing different delicacies to cater to everyone's taste buds. She loved incorporating seasonal fruits and vegetables in her cooking, saying, " The taste of food made from fresh and seasonal produce is unbeatable." So in summers, it was mango mania, with mango being the central ingredient of most dishes. From mango shakes for breakfast, to mango salads, mango chutney, mango curry for lunch to mango souffle for dessert, we were spoilt for choice. As most would agree, mango being the favorite fruit of the majority of Indians including me, no amount was enough. Me and my cousins would often sneak into my grandmother's neighbors garden which had a huge mango tree, in the peak summer afternoons when everyone was enjoying their siesta in chilled AC rooms. With her guard in tow, we would take turns to climb the tree to pluck the biggest and juiciest mangoes. Sitting in the verandah devouring the freshly plucked mangoes with the juice dripping from the sides of our mouths was simply divine. That blissful moment would last till my grandmother's scream, "Did you people even wash your hands before eating?" would jolt us back to reality.

I would then help her prepare her famous mango chutney from some of the raw mangoes we had plucked, which she would send as a thank you gift to her neighbor. Post dinner, we all got to choose our desserts - mango kulfi, mango cheesecake or plain mango. As I would gulp down my last spoon of a succulent mango, savoring its sweet and juicy flavor, there was not a doubt in my mind that the mango truly is the 'king of all fruits'.

🕐 **Preparation time: 10 minutes**
🍲 **Cooking time: 30 minutes**

Ingredients (for 4-5 kulfis)

½ kg milk
50 gms sugar
1 mango
1 slice of white bread
Pinch of cardamom powder
5-6 pistachios

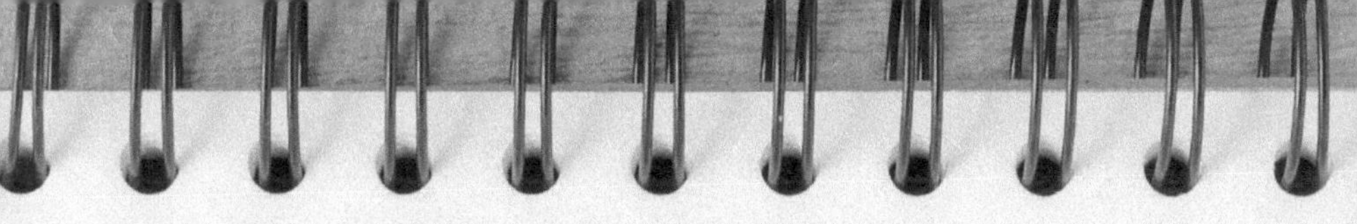

Procedure

1. Take the mango pulp, puree it in a blender and then sieve it till you get a smooth paste.
2. Take the middle part of the bread slice and break it into small pieces.
3. Heat the milk in a pan on slow flame for 15 minutes till it starts to thicken, then add the sugar and cardamom powder.
4. Cook for another 10 minutes till it thickens.
5. Remove from the flame and let it cool.
6. Once it cools add the mango puree and mix well.
7. Transfer the mixture into kulfi moulds and put in the freezer for 5-6 hours.
8. Remove mould from the freezer and open and invert it on a plate and tap gently to take out the kulfi on the plate.
9. Cut the pistachios into thin slices and sprinkle some over the kulfi for decoration.

'Butter Chicken'

Cultural Significance

Butter chicken has come a long way since its accidental origin in a small dhaba in Delhi post partition. It was invented as an efficient way to use leftover chunks of chicken which could not be stored due to lack of refrigeration in those days. The chicken was added to a gravy made of tomatoes, butter and masala and then served to happy customers, giving birth to the present day butter chicken. Over the years, it has crossed boundaries and become globally recognised as one of the most popular Indian dishes. Butter chicken is a staple menu item in North Indian cuisine restaurants, be it small dhabas or fancy fine dining restaurants. The sweetness of its curry along with mildness of spices pleases the palate of young and old alike. Today, it has evolved in a variety of forms such as a filling in sandwiches, pies, rolls, samosas, burgers, as a topping on pizzas and pastas but the classic combination of butter chicken and naan remains undisputed.

Background

Butter Chicken is one of the most popular non vegetarian dishes in North India and a soul food for most Punjabis, our household being no exception. It is a universal favorite, with its creamy, buttery curry which is both savory and sweet. For us, it is both a comfort food as well as a highlight dish for any party. Whenever I feel low and upset, not wanting to eat anything, the sight of butter chicken triggers my happy hormones, making me hungry and salivating once again. In our house, a party menu is complete only after 'the butter chicken' is featured in it. Every Indian restaurant we visit, butter chicken is a must order item. Fun fact: Our most recent trip to the US a couple months ago featured a butter chicken and naan night in Florida!

The same butter chicken tastes different in different restaurants, so having tried it countless times in almost all the restaurants in Delhi, I can confidently say, I do have a favorite! Actually it's more like a family favorite! As they might say, it's in the genes. From my grandparents to my mother and her sibling, to me and my brother, we all seem to have the same taste buds. My grandmother would often tell my brother and me, "You know, years back, when your mother was still very young, there weren't too many eating out options. Out of the few good restaurants, our favorite was one in a nearby market place. Me and your grandfather would often take the children there on special occasions, family celebrations and get togethers with friends. At the restaurant, we would not even look at the menu, and your grandfather would just place the order - butter chicken, butter naan, and makhani dal. The butter chicken was truly a marvel, with succulent pieces of chicken in a rich, creamy aromatic curry. Even though it was the same three items we ate every time, we always came back very satisfied and looking forward to our next visit. You have to try it."

True to her words, once me and my brother tried it, we were hooked on it. Then, due to the pandemic, we were no longer able to order our best loved dish. Seeing our long faces, my grandmother suggested, "Why don't we try to make it at home? It's a great opportunity to learn to make something you love." And there we were: me, my brother and grandmother trying our hand at different butter chicken recipes, giving our own delicious twist and adding to the ever growing breed of home chefs mushrooming during the COVID era. After many trials and retrials, we succeeded in crafting a close second to our favorite butter chicken but soon it took first place for me, because of some of the most unforgettable moments I spent with my grandmother!

🕐 **Preparation time: 30 minutes**
🍲 **Cooking time: 1 hour**

Ingredients

750 gms boneless chicken

For marinade
2 tsp lemon juice
200 gms hung curd

2 tbsp mustard oil

1 tsp salt

1 tbsp ginger garlic paste

1 tsp coriander powder

1 tsp red chili powder

1 tsp cumin powder

½ tsp chaat masala

For curry

750 gms tomatoes

2 big onions

7-8 cloves of garlic

2 inch size pieces of ginger

8-10 cashew nuts

2 sticks of cinnamon

3 green cardamom

2-3 cloves

5-6 whole black peppers

2 green chilis

50 gms butter

5 tbsp oil

100 gms cream

1 tsp kasuri methi (fenugreek leaves)

1 tsp garam masala

1 tsp degi mirch (mild red chili powder)

1 tsp salt

½ tsp sugar

3-4 sprigs of coriander for garnish

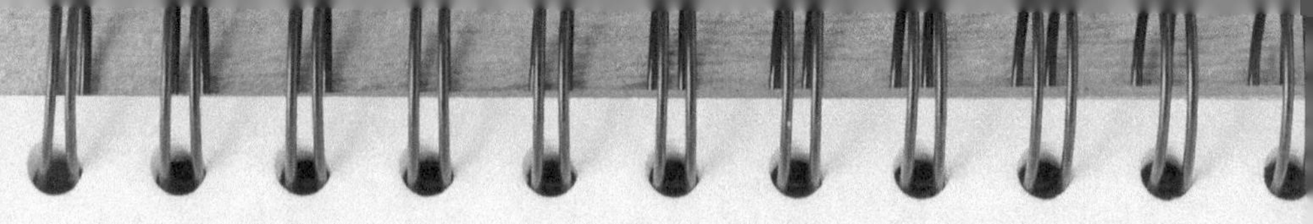

Procedure

1. First marinate the chicken. Cut the chicken into medium sized pieces, wash and dry with a paper towel.

2. Heat the mustard oil till it's lukewarm and then transfer to a bowl. Add the red chili powder and mix it well with the oil.

3. Add the rest of the ingredients to the bowl and mix well to prepare the marinade.

4. Add the chicken pieces to the marinade and give it a good mix. Allow the chicken to marinate for 2-3 hours.

5. While the chicken is marinating, prepare the gravy.

6. Heat 2 tbsp of oil in a pan. Add the whole spices(cinnamon, cloves, black pepper, cardamom) till they start to crackle.

7. Add the chopped tomatoes, chopped onions, ginger, garlic, cashew nuts and green chillis.

8. Cover the pan and cook for 15-20 minutes till the tomatoes and onion are cooked thoroughly and become soft.

9. Allow this mixture to cool, and then remove the cinnamon sticks and blend in a blender to make a paste. Sieve the paste to ensure it is smooth and free of any fibers.

10. In another pan, put 2 tbsp oil and heat it. Add the marinated chicken and cook on high flame first for 5 minutes and then on medium flame for 10-15 minutes.

11. To give a smoky taste to the chicken, take a small bowl, add a piece of hot coal with a spoon of butter on it and place it inside the pan and cover it for 5 minutes.

12. Now to prepare the gravy, take a pan, add the butter and 1 tbsp of oil and heat it.

13. Once hot, add the degi mirch and the tomato onion paste. Cook for 5-7 minutes.

14. Add the salt, garam masala and sugar to the gravy and cook for another 5 minutes.

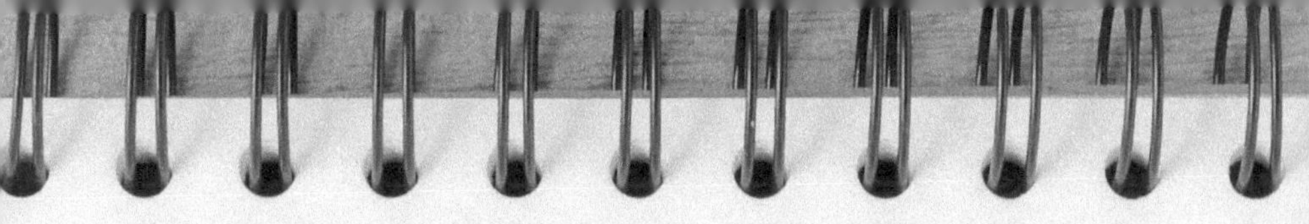

15. Add the cooked chicken pieces. Sprinkle some crushed kasuri methi and add the cream.
16. Cook for another 5 minutes till the chicken pieces get nicely coated with the gravy and the gravy becomes thick and creamy.
17. If you find the gravy to be too thick, you can add some milk and stir it on low flame for 3-4 minutes.
18. Transfer the butter chicken to a bowl and garnish with some cream and coriander if you like.

'Pinni'

Cultural Significance

Pinni is a classic sweet integral to every Punjabi household. Traditionally made with whole wheat flour, ghee, dry fruits and jaggery, it is a powerhouse of strength and energy. It is often given to expectant and new mothers as it supplements their nutrition while they feed their babies. Historically, it was a winter staple in the Punjabi farming community as it was meant to provide energy to the farmers who toiled long hours in the field. However, it soon became an essential part of Punjabi festivals and special occasions, where it was sometimes served as prasad and sometimes as a dessert. Today, many variations are available such as Aate ki pinni, Besan ki pinni, Suji aur ghond ki pinni, each authentic and unique in its own way. Mostly made at home with recipes passed on from one generation to the other, it continues to be the cornerstone of Punjabi culinary traditions.

Background

It was a day before my brother was leaving for university, and a grand farewell dinner was planned at my grandparents house. My grandmother had been busy planning it for days, shortlisting the guest list but still making sure not to miss anyone important among the dozens of relatives, so my brother could receive all the blessings from the elders of the family before he embarked on his journey as a college freshman. After much deliberation, the menu had been finalized which of course included all of my brother's favorite dishes.

As I entered the house early in the evening to help my grandmother with her elaborate preparations, I was instantly drawn to the kitchen by the rich aroma of roasted flour and desi ghee. In there, I find my grandmother all hands on in the kitchen, roasting the flour on the stove, grinding the dry fruits and mixing them together in a big circular bowl. Looking at me she said, "Now, just dont stand there, Ameya, hurry up! I am already late! The guests will be arriving soon and the pinnis have to be ready and packed before that. Time to get your hands dirty! Start mixing the ingredients thoroughly with your fingers and then hand roll it into bite size circular balls. Come quickly, I will show you."

Hesitating for a moment, I washed my hands, rolled up my sleeves and immersed myself in the whole experience of making our traditional family sweet dish. Watching my grandmother and imitating her movements to mix and roll the pinnis with my hands felt cathartic, providing the sensory stimulation that was already making me salivate, a definite benefit of hand-prepared recipes!

Drifting into her childhood memories, my grandmother explained, "When we were young, there weren't many readymade snack options available. Your great grandmother always insisted on homemade food, made with seasonal ingredients which was both nutritious and tasty. So, the onset of winters would be marked with jars of pinnis in our house, ready to be had as breakfast with milk before rushing to school, or as an evening snack after returning from school or simply as a dessert after meals. It's a recipe that I learned from your great-grandmother, have passed on to your mother, and hope to pass on to you as well."

Just as we finished packing the last box, we could hear the bell ring, announcing the arrival of the first guest. Soon the house was reverberating with loud laughter, music and unending conversations. Everyone enjoyed the sumptuous spread prepared by my grandmother and eagerly waited for the long standing ritual of receiving boxes of my grandmother's handmade pinnis. She stood at the exit, happily and proudly distributing boxes of her love and affection to all her near and dear ones as they left, the largest and most special one being for my brother to take with him to university, filled with her love and blessings for a successful and meaningful journey.

🕑 **Preparation time: 10 minutes**

🍲 **Cooking time: 1 hour**

Ingredients (for 15-20 Pinnis)

1 kg whole wheat flour (Atta)

250 gm Gram Flour (Besan)

500 gm Sugar

250 gms Almonds

100 gm Cashew nut

Ghee

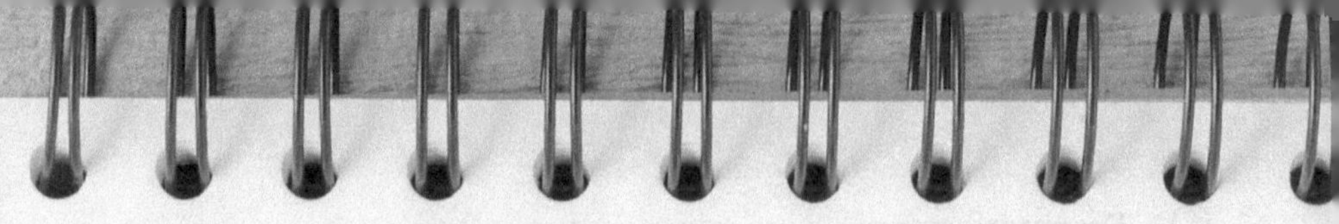

Procedure

1. Heat 100 gms ghee in a pan. Once hot, add the gram flour.
2. Roast it on a slow flame for 15 minutes, till it turns reddish brown.
3. Heat 400 gms ghee in a pan. Once hot, add the whole wheat flour.
4. Roast it on a slow flame for 25 minutes, till it turns reddish brown.
5. Grind the sugar, almonds and cashew nuts in a blender.
6. Allow the roasted whole wheat flour and roasted gram flour to cool.
7. Once it cools, mix both the flours with the sugar and nut mixture together.
8. Mix thoroughly and gently roll the mixture into small balls.
9. Store the balls (pinnis) in an airtight container.

'Chana Dal Khichdi'

Cultural Significance

The origin of the word 'Khichdi' can be traced to the sanskrit word 'khiccha', which refers to a dish cooked with rice and lentils. This dish has been prevalent in India for centuries as is evident from accounts of the many scholars who traveled and explored the Indian subcontinent 14th century onwards. References have been made to the dish in the Indian epic of Mahabharata as well. However, it was during the Mughal period that the dish gained popularity, and was no longer just a humble dish of the common man but a dish that enjoyed royal patronage as well. In Hindu culture, the soft mushy khichdi is often the first solid food fed to infants as it is both easy to digest and nutritious. Today, Khichdi is available in every region of India with its own regional version of the classic dish such as the Bengali khichuri, Tamil pongal, Haryanvi bajra khichri, Odiya adahengu khechidi and Punjabi chana dal khichdi to name a few.

Background

Celebrations were in full swing at the haldi ceremony of my cousin, with the loud sound of dhol (drum beats), the latest Bollywood songs, and nonstop dancing. Brightly colored canopies with a complete marigold theme decoration seemed straight out of a movie set. A traditional haldi ceremony is one of the many momentous pre-wedding events which take place on the morning of the wedding day and is usually attended by close family and friends. The ritual revolves around family members smearing turmeric paste on the bride's and groom's face and hands, while showering them with flowers and blessings. The yellow color of turmeric is synonymous with prosperity in Indian culture and thus, the yellow and orange theme of the ceremony. It was my first time attending such an event and as such, I enjoyed observing each and every ritual that was taking place.

After the endless dancing, just when I was ready to pounce on the delicious lunch spread, I could hear my mother scream, "Wait! Just hold your horses for a bit longer. We have to first make the bride and groom eat some chana dal khichdi and eat some ourselves before lunch. It's a tradition in our family that the khichdi is specially made by the bride's maternal family and served to all the guests for lunch, so you have to help me do that."

I followed her to the kitchen and helped her carry a big cauldron to the dining table. As she lifted the lid, the aroma of the desi ghee and rice filled the room and I tasted the wonder of chana dal khichdi for myself. Yellow in color, it fit the theme and was delicious too. Having two helpings already, I could see my hand stretching out for more, when I had to remind myself that I could not take a chance with my fitted lehenga. Today, I no longer wait for a special occasion to have one of my favorite comfort foods as me and my grandmother are always ready to toss up her famous 'Chana Dal Khichdi'.

🕑 **Preparation time: 45 minutes**
🍲 **Cooking time: 30 minutes**

Ingredients

200 gms rice
300 gms chana dal
2 onions
3 tbsp Ghee
½ tbsp crushed red chilis
1 tsp amchoor (dried mango powder)
1 tsp cumin seeds
¼ tsp ajwain (carom seeds)
½ tbsp coriander powder
¼ tsp dried ginger powder
¼ tsp garlic powder
½ tsp garam masala
1 moti elaichi (black cardamom)
½ tsp lemon juice
Few sprigs of fresh coriander
Salt to taste

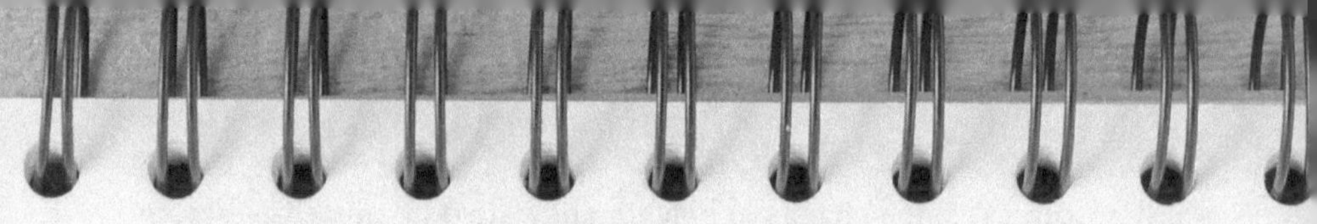

Procedure

1. Boil the rice with ½ tsp of salt in it. Once it is cooked, drain the excess water and set it aside.
2. Soak the chana dal for 30 minutes. Boil the dal with the cardamom and ½ tsp salt, till it softens. Put it aside and let it cool.
3. In a pan, add 2 tbsp of ghee and heat it. Once hot, add cumin and carom seeds.
4. Slice the onions finely and add to the hot ghee. Saute till they soften and turn light brown.
5. Add half the boiled rice and dal to the pan and all the spices except garam masala. Mix together lightly so as to keep the rice intact. Then add the remaining rice and dal, garam masala, a spoon of hot ghee and lemon juice in the end and mix well.
6. Taste for salt and spices; adjust accordingly.
7. Put in a serving bowl and sprinkle some finely chopped coriander on top!

'Chutneys and Pickles'

'Mango Chutney'
'Tamarind Chutney'
'Coriander Chutney'
'Tomato Chutney'
'Green Chilli Pickle'

Cultural Significance

Pickling as a technique for food preservation has been practiced for centuries across different cultures. In Indian culture, the art of pickling represents the culinary legacy of each household where pickle recipes are passed down from one generation to another, with each adding its own special touch. The process of making pickles was traditionally a community activity, with members from the community working together to make large batches of pickles and then distributing them among themselves or even selling them at times. Pickles and chutneys are a significant part of Indian cuisine as they both enhance and balance the flavors of various dishes, adding depth and complexity with their spicy, sour, sweet, or tangy flavors. They also extend the shelf life of seasonal fruits and vegetables and aid in reducing food wastage while also providing numerous health benefits such as anti inflammation and good digestion. Over the years, the tradition of pickling has evolved owing to factors such as region, seasons and availability of raw materials. Pickles and chutneys are often prepared for festivals and special occasions, exchanged as gifts, integrating the community with a sense of harmony and kinship.

Background

As I sat at the dining table quietly eating my lunch, I tried my hardest to control my smile, which was starting to appear at the corners of my mouth. I could see myself flinching under my brother's angry stare from across the table. He was being reprimanded by my grandmother, "You are such a fussy eater. Why don't you eat any healthy food? No fruits, no vegetables. You only want to eat junk food all the time. Look at Ameya! She eats all the vegetables that are cooked at home, be it bottle gourd, brinjal, pumpkin, or spinach. Never has she complained once about what is made for lunch or dinner. Learn something from her." As she showered me with heaps of praises, I could feel my brother turning green with envy. After lunch, as my brother and I retreated to our room, he sat in a corner, sulking and refusing to talk to anyone.

Later at night, once he had calmed down, I decided to help him. "Let me tell you the secret behind being able to eat any vegetable that is made at home. It is not that I like every vegetable, but I pair it with one of the chutneys or pickles that nani makes, and their sweet, tangy, spicy flavors just make every dish tasty, delicious, and mouthwatering. They are a perfect appetizing and flavorsome accompaniment to any dish. You should try it!" I shared. Soon enough, I found my advice being adhered to, and my brother was relishing some of my grandmother's mango chutney with a potato and brinjal vegetable for lunch. I couldn't help noticing the smile beaming on my grandmother's face watching him eat his vegetables, and her gentle nod at me as I caught her eyes said it all!

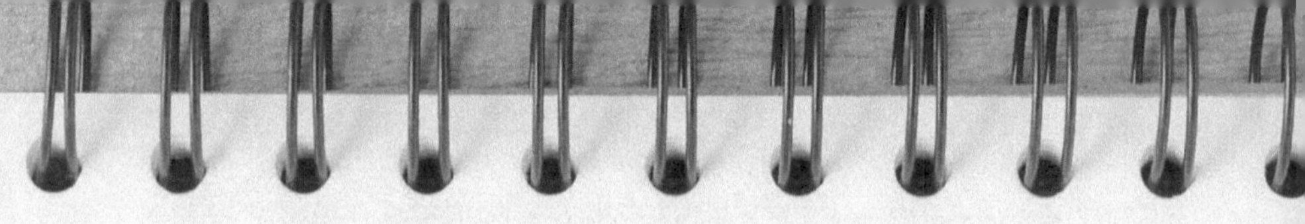

Mango Chutney:

🕐 **Preparation time: 10 minutes**

🍲 **Cooking time: 20 minutes**

Ingredients

2 raw mangoes

100 gm sugar

1 tsp panch phoron mixture(five spice blend)

2 tbsp oil

¼ tsp black salt

1 tsp salt

Procedure

1. Peel and grate the mangoes.
2. Heat the oil in a frying pan. Once hot, add the panch phoron mixture.
3. Once the mixture starts to crackle, add the grated mango, sugar and salt.
4. Cover and cook on slow flame for about 15 minutes.
5. Keep stirring the contents in the pan so that it doesn't burn and stick to the bottom of the pan.
6. Remove from the pan once the mango is cooked and turns soft and pulpy.
7. Allow it to cool and store in an airtight container.
8. Note - Panch phoron mixture consists of cumin seed (jeera), nigella seed (kalonji), fenugreek seed (methi), brown mustard(rai) and fennel seed(saunf)in equal parts.

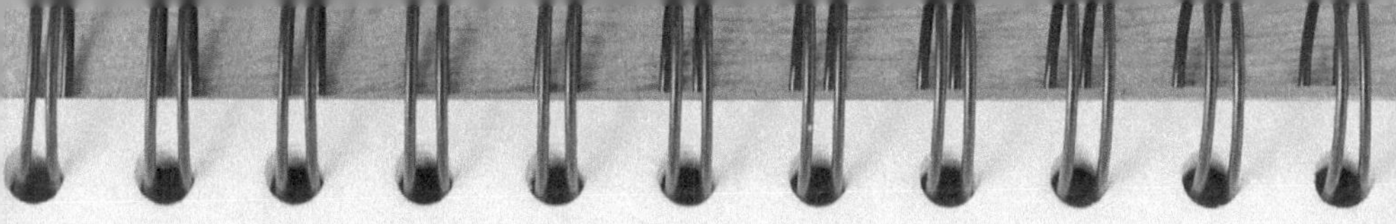

Tamarind Chutney:

🕑 **Preparation time: 20 minutes**

🍲 **Cooking time: 40 minutes**

Ingredients

100 gms Tamarind deseeded

150 gms sugar or jaggery

½ tsp red chili powder

½ tsp roasted cumin powder

1 tsp coriander powder

1 tsp of salt

1/4 tsp of black salt

1 tsp of chaat masala

Pinch of asafoetida (hing)

Procedure

1. Soak the Tamarind in water for 15 minutes.
2. Mash the tamarind with your hand and sieve the mixture.
3. Roast the cumin seeds till they turn slightly brown and give their aroma, then grind them to a fine powder.
4. Cook the tamarind pulp with all the other ingredients for half an hour on slow flame stirring it continuously till it thickens.
5. If you find it too thick, you can add some water while cooking the pulp.
6. Let the chutney cool and then transfer to a glass jar and refrigerate.

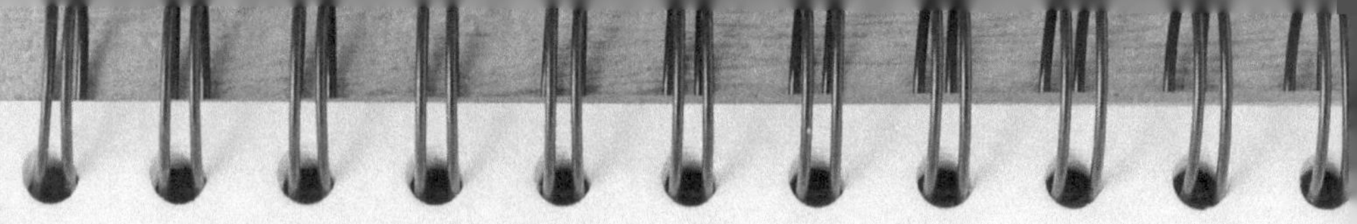

Coriander Chutney:

🕑 **Preparation time: 10 minutes**
🍲 **Cooking time: 10 minutes**

Ingredients

100 gms coriander leaves with tender stalks
3-4 sprigs of mint leaves
1 amla (gooseberry) or half a raw mango or 1 tbsp lemon juice
Pinch of sugar
½ tsp salt
1 tsp cumin powder
1-2 green chilies

Procedure

1. Rinse the coriander and mint nicely under running water and then drain the excess water.
2. Chop the coriander and mint leaves coarsely.
3. Cut the gooseberry/raw mango into small pieces.
4. Add all the ingredients to a blender jar and blend till you get a fine paste.
5. In case you find the chutney too thick, you may add 2-3 tbsp of water.
6. Adjust the salt, chillies and lemon juice according to taste.
7. Store in a glass jar in the refrigerator.

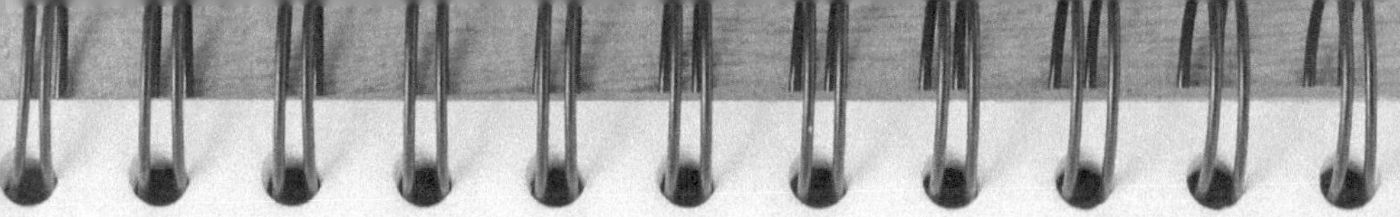

Tomato Chutney:

🕑 **Preparation time: 10 minutes**

🍲 **Cooking time: 25 minutes**

Ingredients

250 gms red tomatoes

1 tsp panch phoron mixture

2 dried red chili

½ tsp degi mirch (mild red chili powder)

¼ tsp turmeric powder

3 tbsp mustard oil

2 tbsp sugar

10-12 raisins

1 tsp salt

Procedure

1. Heat the oil in a pan.
2. Once hot, add the dried red chilis and the panch phoron mixture, till it crackles.
3. Cut the tomatoes into small pieces and add to the pan.
4. Then add the salt, turmeric powder, degi mirch powder and stir.
5. Cover the pan and cook for 10-15 minutes till the tomatoes become mushy.
6. Add the sugar and raisins and cook for another 5-7 minutes till the sugar dissolves completely.
7. Turn off the flame and allow the chutney to cool before transferring to an airtight glass container.
8. Refrigerate for future use upto a week to ten days.

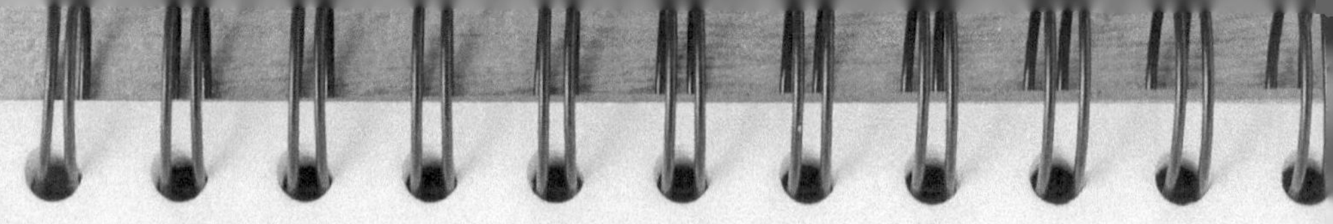

Green Chilli Pickle:

🕐 **Preparation time: 15 minutes**

🍲 **Cooking time: 20 minutes**

Ingredients

100 gms green chilis

3 tsp coriander powder

1 tsp salt

¼ tsp red chili powder

1 tsp amchoor (dried mango powder)

1 tsp panch phoran

½ tsp haldi (turmeric powder)

½ tsp ground fresh fennel

6-7 tbsp mustard oil

1 tsp jaggery coarsely ground

Pinch of hing (asafoetida)

Procedure

1. Chop the green chilis into small pieces.
2. Heat 3-4 tbsp of mustard oil on slow fire and once hot, add pinch of hing and the panch phoran mixture.
3. Turn off the flame and then add the rest of the ingredients. Mix well till the jaggery melts.
4. Heat 2-3 tbsp of mustard oil for 5 minutes and let it cool.
5. Transfer the chili mixture in a glass jar and pour the cooled oil on top of it till all the chilis are fully soaked and there is a layer of oil on top.
6. Keep it aside for 2-3 days and it is ready for use!

Epilogue

Heartfelt reflections

As you turn the final page of this book, I want to thank you for joining me on this journey of exploring the rich interplay between flavors, stories and cultural traditions that I will treasure forever. What began as a document to record precious memories of my grandmother's life has blossomed into something far more profound. Writing 'A Pitara of Love' has been my small effort to ensure that my sweet nani's recipes and stories are preserved for generations to come. The dishes in this book are inspired by a symphony of emotions, unforgettable moments between my grandmother and I, and stories that I've acquired throughout my life. Each page is infused with the memories of our shared moments of laughter, learning and the bittersweet reality of her illness.

As I write the last page, I am filled with an overwhelming sense of joy, but also a pinch of sadness, as I realize the journey of writing this book has come to an end. It has been a cherished excuse to spend countless hours with my grandmother in the kitchen. Her kitchen was my first classroom, where I learnt the true meaning of creativity, innovation, discipline, patience and most importantly, love. This journey has also been a revelation, teaching me so much about my culture that I didn't know before!

Thus, I urge you to create your own memories each time you step into the kitchen. Whatever your mood and whatever you are craving, you'll find ample recipes to try: whether you prepare the Pinnis, Chutneys, or Kabuli Pulao, I hope you reawaken your love for food as you indulge in these dishes that are as nourishing for your body as they are for your soul!

So, what are you waiting for?

Get started and create your own tales for generations to come!

Doli Ki Roti

Phirni

Pani Puri

Jalebi

Chocolate Halwa

Lemon Drizzle Cake

Kabuli Pulao

Sindhi Kadhi

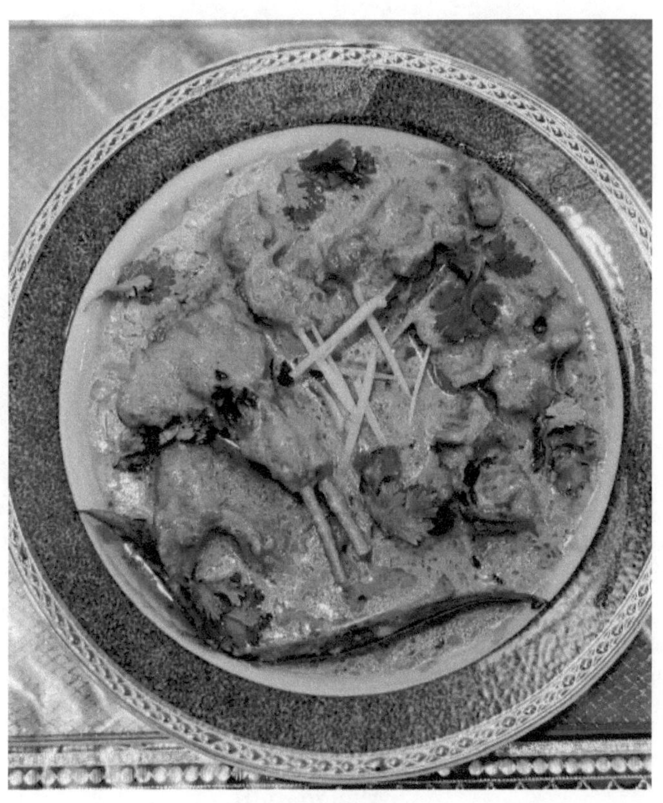

Roganjosh

Apple Pie

Mango Kulfi

Butter Chicken

Pinni

www.ingramcontent.com/pod-product-compliance
Lightning Source LLC
LaVergne TN
LVHW050416160726
843469LV00041B/1098